TO:

HAPPY BIRTHDAY

GUEST GUEST

THOUGHTS THOUGHTS

GUEST   GUEST

THOUGHTS   THOUGHTS

GUEST	GUEST
THOUGHTS	THOUGHTS

GUEST GUEST

THOUGHTS THOUGHTS

GUEST   *GUEST*

THOUGHTS   *THOUGHTS*

GUEST　　　　　GUEST

THOUGHTS　　　THOUGHTS

PHOTOS

PHOTOS

PHOTOS

PHOTOS

PHOTOS

Printed in Great Britain
by Amazon